Love, from the ends of the earth

for Rosemary Deen
in thanks for your encouragement —
Enoch Dillon 10-12-90

Love, from the ends of the earth

Enoch Dillon

Fithian Press ❖ Santa Barbara, California ❖ 1990

Several of these poems in the same or slightly altered versions have appeared or will appear elsewhere. Grateful acknowledgment is made to the following: *Poet Lore, Visions, Gryphon, Poultry, Country Cottage Poetry Journal, The San Fernando Poetry Journal, The Federal Poet, Heaven Bone, Earthwise,* and *Three Apples Fell,* Bruce Fleming, Editor.

I would like to thank Mary Greene Seymour, Dolores MacKenna, Cornelia Veenendaal, and JoAnn Nolen for their appreciation and critique of many of these poems. Also I am grateful to Ann Darr; Seamus Heaney; Phillip Jason; Rod Jellema; Denise Levertov; The Writer's Center, Bethesda, MD; The Federal Poets, Washington, DC; The James Joyce Summer School, Dublin, Ireland; and The Yeats International Summer School, Sligo, Ireland for workshops and programs in which some of this poetry originated.

Cover: aerial photo by Enoch Dillon of the Grand Canyon at junction of Colorado and Little Colorado rivers.

Copyright © 1990 by Enoch Dillon
All rights reserved
Printed in the United States of America

LIBRARY OF CONGRESS CATALOGING-IN-PUBLICATION DATA

Dillon, Enoch, 1925-
    Love, from the ends of the earth : poems / by Enoch Dillon
      p.   cm.
    ISBN 0-931832-64-0 : $7.50
    I. Title
    PS3554.I419L68   1990
    811' .54--dc20   90-3627
                                              CIP

CONTENTS

GUIDE FOR THE PERPLEXED

Recipe	10
Great Chain of Being	11
Jogging on St. Stephen's Green	12
Perspective	13
Guide for the Perplexed	14
The World as Substance and Solecism	15
Amelia Earhart and the Generation Gap	16
On an Early Death	17
First Love	18
The Economic Interpretation of History	19
The Interpretation of Dreams	20
A Genie is not Amused	21
A Grammar for Assent	22
Civilization and its Detritus	23
The Truth about Hester Thrale and Samuel Johnson	24
Jogging with Gottschalk	25
Yeats and the Utilitarians	26
Telling My Granddaughter about the Tillamook Burn	28
Saint Teresa's Pool	30
On Being Questioned by Socrates' Ghost in the Agora	30
Gland Opera	31
The World as Wish and Wisdom	32

NEGATIVE ASHES

Negative Ashes	34
Deja Vu	36
Relativity	36
A Golden String	37
Love, from the ends of the earth	38
A Psalm for the Swamp Along 104	39
A Commentary on Hopkins' *Inscape*	40

Credo	40
Faith in Venice	41
No Sanctuary	42
Teas for Two	43
Time Present by Northwest	44
Endangered Species	45
The Gorge	46
Peacock	48
Spectator Sport	48

BUOYANCY

Latitudinarian	50
Poem Without Ending	51
Sunday Matins	52
Coda	53
In Defense of Adam	54
Sundial	55
Meteora, Greece	56
A Gloss on the Gloaming	57
Heritage	58
Daughters of Elysium	59
The End of the Ice Age	59
Lauds in the Algarve	60
"You Must Change Your Life."	61
Oregon Agate	62
Asperges Night	63
Buoyancy	64

Dedicated to my children:
Mary, Thomas, Maura, John,
Rose Marie, and Miriam

GUIDE FOR THE PERPLEXED

This is my letter to the World

—*Emily Dickinson*

RECIPE

Read the cookbook
for a sense of substance
and proportion.

Saute diced chicken
with little fat
or garnished skin.

Add finely shredded bay
basil or rosemary
depending on the moon

not counting teaspoons
but what the texture
obscurely demands.

Stir in tomato sauce
mushrooms from the swamp
and oil of olive.

Simmer till the owl
with lots of garlic
stingily adding oil

till the bubbles
shine like the sun
on fool's gold.

Serve with rigatoni
salting lightly
if not angry.

GREAT CHAIN OF BEING

In tropical rain forests
a million species slant
or spawn on roots and sun

a billion-year experiment
in reciprocity and coexistence
air, water, earth against fire

breeding smoke and ash
leaving tentative topsoil
to wash away in minutes

few trees to smell sky
and send it back clean
inspiring humans
who haven't lived here long.

JOGGING ON ST. STEPHEN'S GREEN
(for Dolores MacKenna, Dublin 8-27-88)

My wind aches, my grace is creaking
down Harcourt Street as I pass around
two Russian women and a man
heading for Trinity. Outside the Green
I pick up stride towards Grafton Street
the guard just opening the gates
marked *Fir* and *Mna*.

Some say we joggers grit our teeth
and grunt, but I smile at early bards
then laugh as I remember Joyce's
"Saint Anonymous" after forty-five years:

My English teacher couldn't get me
to stop reading and pay attention
so said, "Read *Ulysses* and report."
I read and read and read a key
and knew of Molly Bloom before
I knew of woman. I never thought I'd
run one day with Joyce remembering
that English teacher as she was in 1942.

I circle past the Russians photographing
Countess Markievicz's bust this millennium
of Dublin's birth and Russian Christianity.

Gliding with second wind, I glimpse sun
and pray past Newman's chapel: I hope
for Glasnost, but I know this evening
I'll be waiting with an English teacher
                        for Godot at the Gate.

PERSPECTIVE

September stills hunger
raining red apples
the sweetest meridian striped
and with luck Father
brings trout for supper
from the Tualatin.

What's poker with toothpicks?
The cover has ripped
from our baseball—
the schoolyard track's
a continent away.
Hours trudge past
resident landlords
where stores with fading
Blue Eagles seem mislaid
from a richer planet.

Apples we couldn't eat
nor Mother can for winter
cuddled in loamy earth.
With sticks of kindling
punched into apples
we swung wide arcs
whipped our wrists
and smashed our lumps
against Harlan Crabbe's
abandoned barn,

    never foreseeing luck
    circumnavigate fifty years
    and return to jog
    around town in twelve minutes—
    a distance not too much farther
    than you can throw an apple.

GUIDE FOR THE PERPLEXED

Sleeping late on a mizzly morning
        rhythm fondling the roof
                I rest, the rain works

washing obsessive muddles.

Rising I find the Daily Echo
too damp to read.

If you want to recover
how the world's reborn

      just once

           sleep in,

                  dream,

and don't read the morning paper.

THE WORLD AS SUBSTANCE AND SOLECISM

This morning's sun rose archly from the west.
A cardinal I named Narcissus preens,
begs seed while burping from his swollen breast—
pert squirrels steal despite my quarantines.

My wife's away to daughter's house to knit
while I weave words best left to jesting bards.
My son brings Kate whose three-year nimble wit
precludes the art of analysing words to shards.

I try to write—she pounds piano keys
then marigolds a Sesame Street mouse
on drafts of pity poems about damp trees.
I ask her how she likes her Grandma's house—

her stomping and her repartee make clear:
"This isn't Grandma's house, Grandma isn't here."

AMELIA EARHART AND THE GENERATION GAP

My daughter named granddaughter Sally Ride—
not Gabriela, Emily, Denise,
Elizabeth, or Anna. If she wanted
a technology Terpsichore,
why not Amelia?

        MacArthur once
directed me to search the Solomons
for a PT Commander Kennedy.
The Papuans who on Coral Island heard
no epic clash of vessels in the night
once saw a flaming phaeton with Goddess
asking sacrifice of virgin boars
and missionary Bibles.

        Jungle Island
stragglers of retreating Japanese
spoke of a photographing spy, almost
invincible, who was shot down but then
seduced the General.

        Melanesians on
Lost Atoll rumored that a fair Gauguin,
fed up with husband, fans, and Reagan films,
had married a fat Chieftain on far sands
and matriarched twelve brats and concubines.

I never came across the rich man's son
nor the barnstorming muse from airy Kansas.
Sally Ride will not get lost in space,
but if she should, would poets fashion legends
as they did about Amelia?

ON AN EARLY DEATH

Touching bark of a Sitka spruce
which dwarfs some seven centuries
I meditate on roots of earth
straining to regain the heavens.

A butterfly has passed by
lambent even in this misty forest
ephemeral colors as salient
as a supernova's nuclear fire.

No canvas caught the butterfly
whose wings had barely budged the air
although the spruce's fall would echo
even in an empty forest.

Did this evergreen seem eternal
to Nehalem before Columbus sailed?
Did they doubt or pray for transients,
or wonder meaning of a flutter?

Uneasiness leads me to questions
about ambiguous frescoes of being
where we admire spruce and stars
as if they owned life, or time were constant,

for like the butterfly I wing aspiring
beyond the cosmos of earth's canvas
to where black holes reverse and time
no longer shrouds each moment.

FIRST LOVE
(for Jean Dillon)

I was born to apples
hitching posts
and sod houses.

I carried rifles
and slept with ferns
long before I knew phones.

When rainbows paled
I read nursery rhymes
by coal oil lamps.

And each season
the sun stolen south
may never return.

Now all my gods
are dead, robotized
or in process.

I'm lobotomized
by binary blackmail
and non-bank banks.

I don't want to live
in a neologized world
without books or letters

nor prioritize star wars
mechanical hearts
and feelsmart pills.

Yet at each moon's waning
I remember the jet
that took me to you.

THE ECONOMIC INTERPRETATION OF HISTORY

"Sir," Samuel Johnson usually
prefixed to pontification:
"No man but a blockhead
ever wrote except for money."
The world must be wallowing
with the wages of dullness—
we unread computer poets
flood a wasteland of readers
but are lionized as bards
carrying our mirrors about
closer than wit and riddle.
It has not been reported
that Doctor Johnson earned
a tidy sum for *Vanity*.

THE INTERPRETATION OF DREAMS

I started an affair
with this blonde, built
like Dolly Parton, wearing
matching yellow toque.

An unsteady flasket
she stood on a table
replacing a burnt-out bulb.
Screwing done, she stepped

to a chair-back, spilled
down looming stairs
rolling head over fanny
to flatten on the floor below.

I felt beneath her breast
asking where she hurt:
"Just bruised this time."
I woke and flushed my pills.

A GENIE IS NOT AMUSED

If whiskey were words
I'd long ago have explained
the behavior of the bourgeoisie

for I carried my typewriter
to an underground press
in taverns of triviality

where self-pity sucked in gravity—
the few cries of creation leaden
with a passion that couldn't rise.

Liquid lobotomy no longer loosed
my unconscious censor—
no dreams escaped my black hole.

The bourgeoisie did very well without me.

I panicked when my genie was capped
(yes, you *can* bottle the genie back)
and bitching replaced bourbon

for I had lost the spirit of drunks
the inspiration of doom and denial.
Months followed fallow in a green hole,

till Thalia said, "Write, write with dry wit
you can play libel lawyer
and censor of smut later

as long as the few brain cells
you have remaining
are left free to be contradicted."

A GRAMMAR FOR ASSENT
(*Viewing Strick's* Ulysses, *James Joyce Summer School,
Newman House, Dublin, 1989*)

What was haunting us that twilight
lovers elsewhere, lonelyhearted fancies
                    or witchcraft of Mnemosyne?

Following Poldy through Dublin to Molly
watching a peripatetic cuckold home to a *yes*
                  surviving the quotidian

yes ending the film, darkening, silence,
credits start against background music:
"Love's Old Sweet Song." A low hum
some said chanced within a priest
(did he know something we did not?)
till all seemed chanting vernal vespers—
                  there's hope back home.

Out in the courtyard purple paints
a candelabra of branches. A leaven
of leaves blankets a concrete Neptune
like a tamer sea. The citizen mutters
"...Old Sweet Schmaltz," twisting his tongue
refusing to admit a word like *love*
                  into the contemporary.

Obscuring night, a magpie meanders into dreams.

CIVILIZATION AND ITS DETRITUS

Trash-man.
Greater than god my father
arching our garbage bounty
up in that compactor's jaws
surer than Kareem Abdul-Jabbar.

Sunbrown biceps, sunnier grin,
glowing from labor's craft
taking away our glut of affluence
waste cabbage, diapers and secrets.

At Christmas father would have me
give him a fiver.

When I grew up
he carried away love letters
fit for blackmail or biography
and even later my empty bottles
hidden in bags of garbage
till a raven smelling rot
tore them apart for neighbors to see.

The FBI spies on our trash
while flying saucers carry Elvises
in methane up from swampy dumps
and counties fight for rubbish sites
for junk mail, bonds and prose
assuring us atomic wastes will radiate
but only for ten thousand years.

People don't pride the Institute
for Advanced Waste Management
or hope their kids grow up
to be Refuse Reprocessors:
it takes a lot of grit
to carry out the trash
from five billion people.

THE TRUTH ABOUT HESTER THRALE AND SAMUEL JOHNSON

Of all the writers past
I read no closer friends
than Sam and Hester cast
romantic till the end.

At end starved Hester wails
we're thirty years apart,
so blame the guest of the Thrales
for she's no middle-aged tart.

She serves a straying spouse,
twelve children, and this wit
(now garrulous old grouse
whose stay is infinite).

Her oldest daughter, Queenie,
bosses her around.
Her Henry's not a meanie,
but mistresses abound.

Though her devotion tires
sage Sam to her owes debts
for with her care he sires
Lives of the English Poets.

When Henry dies of booze,
obesity, and stroke,
Sam Johnson wants his muse,
but Hester wants no yoke—

for now she's freedom's creature,
although Sam pleads with tropes:
with Queenie's music teacher,
Piozzi, she elopes.

JOGGING WITH GOTTSCHALK

They said
he was dead
along with God,
his groupies dead,
his dying poets fallen
in gilt Victorian parlors.
Now to anthem and cakewalk themes
flamboyantly lightfooting from the Caribbean,
those tropic nights floating, I, God's rogue, scamper
downhill with tailwind, Euterpe, silver shoes, and yes even
his groupies, gliding, striding, soaring for one moment singing
the harmony of grace, ground, Gottschalk and all the galloping spheres.

YEATS AND THE UTILITARIANS

Full of Yeats and fancied youth, I ride
the Dublin train from Sligo, sitting across
from farmer and young wife on holiday.

He mumbles on each stone-fenced farm
viewing his universe of cattle and rich soil.
She sparkles while looking for an opening—

"Why did you visit Sligo?" she asks this alien
poet manque flaunting his American west,
a bolo tie with agate hanging from his throat.

Trying to impress her, I declare that I'm
a burnt-out economist now writing poetry.
She wonders why most farmers are so poor.

"Excess production and inelastic demand"
I babble, but she, with gambit grin, ripostes:
"Bureaucrats who never shoveled shit."

Her diversions come from television—
she asks about the salaries paid the stars.
"Very little," I say, "just a few at the top

make capitalist salaries." I couldn't duck
her hidden pitchfork rising from the earth:
"Then how can they afford so many wives?"

My bolo clasps its agate of cerise and salmon
pluming upwards to blue and yellow sky—
she says it looks like painting on ceramic.

I hand her the bolo, the old man wary,
and tell her the agate story, chalcedony
that alchemized a million years in crucibles

beneath Oregon beaches—ten thousand more
prehistoric years for Mother Nature to paint
its translucent shaman chanting Indian stories:

Graveyard Point giants from volcanic caverns
throwing picaresque rocks, now under driftwood
from vessels crashed on headlands of the gods.

He fingers his dark brown holiday tie: "Cost me
five pounds." She caresses the once-fabled agate:
                      "It does the job," she says.

TELLING MY GRANDDAUGHTER
ABOUT THE TILLAMOOK BURN

Hot easterns dried Nehalem's rocks; young deer
scrounged for water. Oregon's ever green grass
decayed to khaki, brush to tinder.
Joe Lamper claimed he saw a mountain lion
prowl in moonlight on Vernonia's street.
But why believe him when he told his story
years after Tillamook's tall forest burned.

Your great-grandmother loved those rare clear days
when washing dried within the hour. The sun
would briefly drug us till life's rain returned
and Wilson's loam spawned milk and berries.

The Douglas fir roots searched for water but
found flint instead. Some camper left a spark
or, though logging had been banned, some shark
dragged the last log for ready cash.
Others say the fire was intentional—
fire fighting jobs for Clatsop's unemployed.

A common summer forest fire forged
by August twenty-fourth of thirty-three,
a furnace large as Okinawa
and ashed four hundred years of growth, the smoke
too dense to augur any mushroom clouds.

I stopped playing catch in the midnight noon;
your one-month old great-Aunt Donna gagged
in so much smoke. That night a caravan
of Model Ts and As crawled down the hills.

I still remember panic, and toy pistol,
symbol of my manhood, lost that night
as was your great-grandfather's logging job.

September ocean rains then damped the fury,
falling apples filled depression bellies,
but salmon found the forest rivers lye,
worms ate charcoal, the deer had furled fossil,
the mills heard ghosts of birds and donkey engines.

In July of forty-five, fresh from Fort Benning
I stopped en route to the Philippines.
The fire had returned, charcoal stumps and brush
glow-burned ten miles west from Gales Creek
where swimming, Eve and I ignored the fire.
          Further to the west
Manila sintered rubble. One building survived
the fires in Nagoya—and Hiroshima
would live just three more weeks.

But what did I care then about ecology,
disarmament or unemployment?
Eve had come home from Stanford to an empty car
and I held ration cards for gasoline.

SAINT TERESA'S POOL

Liquid diamond sunning

Filigree floor rocking

Foam in chorus spiring

I butterfly in God.

ON BEING QUESTIONED
BY SOCRATES' GHOST IN
THE AGORA

Socrates still springs
among these knolls,
where he wouldn't buy things
but stole men's souls.

GLAND OPERA

"Not understanding Italian, I thought the music beautiful until
Signora Lucia explained that the Duke took advantage of Rigoletto's
daughter. Out in Arizona we call that rape."
—Senator Harlan Crabbe, 1895.

See the bass bare   dirty teeth dear
spare your hair   bat's sticky wing
valkyries sing   Wagner's fear dear
fey nightmare   of the Ring.

Opera mixes   grimmest story
ballet guilt   gory nations
fondles divas   with no glory
never ever   liberations.

Garish foyers   glaze and reek out
blending jasmine   and cigar
but bored patrons   blithely sneak out
from passions   most bizarre.

Dare you dine   on cacciatore
cut by Mack's   sharpened knives
share the cell   in Trovatore
flagrant votives   vagrant wives?

If you dislike   bloody curios
classic rape   and drunken vermin
bare just beauty   on your stereos
sans Italian   French and German.

THE WORLD AS WISH AND WISDOM

I heard the owl

at dawn's theophany

hooting in the haunted wood

that barely a third of life

is dealt in dreams.

NEGATIVE ASHES

*"Hope" is the thing with feathers
That perches in the soul—*

—Emily Dickinson

NEGATIVE ASHES

Across the bay from Yeats's Tomb
I photograph a dune precisely cut
revealing layers of clam shells

a ten-century garbage dump
for clambakes once chanted
by a thousand willie yeatses.

Away from scent of seaweed
I slog through mud and dung
uphill to deeper lore

past cattle that sentinel
dolmens and passage graves
that once caged vatic ashes.

A latter-day stone-ager
disturbing crypts of faith
and theology sculpt in stone

I think autochthons do not count
and focus on us curious Celts
among those living dead

whose history is read in cromlechs.
Crawling in a passage grave
where bare walls also psalm a story

my camera calls out to bards
who ate smaller clams each year
and vanished with their words.

I scribble this like tendriled kelp
on paper salvaging the time
for my film sleeps fallow like the grave

enchanted by the people's goddess
who had never invited me
to savage her etchings.

DEJA VU

As the first lichen

spread over the sintered rubble

God said, "Dummkopf.

This time learn the difference

between saving your arse

and your arsenals."

RELATIVITY

Faint birth of flint

blinding fifteen billion

years before Yorick

reds rainbow in my lens

and basks fast forward

to shadow beyond cuckoo

my Swiss bank account.

A GOLDEN STRING

I chant half-lotus in the dark
to search for veiled skeins of ore
that alchemized before the furthest star.

Befriended by an earthy chorus
I breathe within to reach beyond
"God one, God two, God three, God four."

A pious trance, cliched mirages,
anxieties to come next August
contend against this sacred pause.

"God grins, God's grace, God ninety-nine"—
one hundred moments each a sprite
who carries truth in fabled fire.

No moment's ever lost Blake said.
Woolgathering days that salvage shards
in time will hallow every gilded yarn.

Love, from the ends of the earth

Angles of sun and shadow

rust the Grand Canyon

where the Little Colorado

turquoises past arroyos

and the earth mothers

mesas of mystery

older than angels.

A PSALM FOR THE SWAMP ALONG 104

The swamp hangs witching in VanHendrick's woods,
a secret clothed with mystery and spawners
curtained from the heavens by mists and firs.

These foreign chambers challenge my nine years,
but curiosity succeeds the fear of sudden
as flushed pheasants pound their panic into rush.

From under an old shed where once a hobo lived
a hundred garters flee my halting steps, stripes
snapping their survival from primordial judgment.

The young skunks reek after their play—
trout search for rivers from compost creeks—
spring's sperm renews the fern and fungus—
erotic trilliums droop with blight.

Teeming, rutting, lilting, rotten, sprouting—
this Sylvan cesspool feeds worms, bugs, and slugs
lauding new life's errant elan.

Walking home God argues that all makes sense
(later, that my life is connected to every other life)
but I get tanned for muddy shoes.

A COMMENTARY ON HOPKINS' INSCAPE

My left sock is unique—

I've worn a hole in it.

God's love wills each mystique

for even voids show wit.

CREDO

I once believed that every topaz
was lustered yellow, freezing my
secure enjoyment of God's certainties—

in this chameleon world a fix of stone
to stellar principle, until this adamant
had also learned that spots of earth

mutate, that stars and quarks perplex,
yet on behavior I am God's geologist
who never has erupted into doubt.

FAITH IN VENICE

From the Lido the vaporetto
bounces through spindrift salty
with byzantine opulence

of Grand Canal palaces
that laud old masters
money and expatriates

to Saint Mark's Square
where I perch a fledgling pigeon
and become repentant Doge

praying near that dark basilica
where votive candles vaporized
the credo of my youth

leaving Adriatic floods
under the catwalk from Saint Mark's—
oh for the eyes of Canaletto.

NO SANCTUARY

Oh, if John Calvin's awful God
were too sulfurous to slake,
what about the Christian one?

Will our crystal hermitage survive
flood, famine, quake and virus
aching voices of cynical passives
belief in cycles, fate and lapses?

Someday even we forgetful fakes,
safe by spirits, gun and cheap labor,
may be seduced by an artful God
staking choices, choices, choices...

TEAS FOR TWO

Steeping *gunpowder green* unfolds
tentacles groping down drowsy
pyrex teapot, as delicate hope

rises from steaming water
to rest in fresh desire—
scent of an empire.

Dark-eyed *darjeeling* caressed
from bushes stiffened by monsoons
and the burning god of forgetting

fondles fate with scones and jam
though all's an obscure dream
pouring another metamorphosis.

Jasmine blossoms in twilight zen
unaware of not-otherness
tao of perfumed gardens—

lucent cups greengold
languish without a ripple
on this flaccid world.

TIME PRESENT BY NORTHWEST

Basaltic rock outcropped raw on time's ridge
two hundred million years before Cascades
erupted westward. Twenty million years
matured the Douglas firs and loams and deer
to rear us simple owners of this earth
ten thousand years ago. Though even now
Olympics crack, man's eighty years erode,
and sintering hours turn volcanic ash,

all will survive, accumulating time
beyond primeval stone. While crags decay
the world evolves Pacific's embryo
in craters quaking with elan itself

abducting human flint from lithic dust
sun's twilight westward with a frontier lust.

ENDANGERED SPECIES
(Over 700 years old, Oregon)

This Sitka spruce raised heaven's roots before
a grimmer woods discovered Dante lost.
Surviving quakes, fires, and enterprise
while nurtured by volcanic ash and snows,
it hallows husbandry and prays to feed
my meditation. Overhead careens
a seven-hundred-mile-an-hour jet
chalking space but never chafing time.

Some day this welkin tree will rhyme more pulp
than all our poets need, more songs than jets
that macho-Mach across Nehalem shrines.

A poet-prophet lived for half this age
and walked one day with God. We learn no more:
he had forgotten to touch earth and write.

THE GORGE

The Columbia bubbles from Canadian Rockies
murmurs through sagebrush into the Gorge
where basalt rapids swash rain and leaves.
The predestined desert from the fallow east
abruptly turns to rainbow dynasties
of roots, apples, rhododendrons, fir and deer.

A stone bridge once spanned the Gorge,
commerce between north and south,
till mountain gods on Helens and Hood
threw thunder eggs at one another
sinking the bridge, purifying the fatherland.

The burnished north side of the Gorge
survives in warrior dreams of youthful dare
roulette in the river's vortices
fortune surviving on a chancy spit.

The Cascades on the sunless side erupted
in the great upheaval of meaning, the river
washing memory to aging west and brine.
These palisades are no sunny paradise
to weaken even the meek
but damp daylong twilight
silvered by waters of maidens tumbling—
blown mist, horsetail, bridal veil—
moonbeams where the moon herself
is only inferred from shadows.

Today the cankered gods are quiet
as they rid the westerlies of rain
sequestering waters for survivors'
inheriting roots against capricious winds—
green unravelling a gordian cosmos.

While firtops stretch for rainbows
above millennia of basalt beds
where neither wonder nor imagination
could spawn moss or whiten the trillium,
persistence reigns in the Gorge—
pacific havens mulch its silting script.

PEACOCK

You think that old beard,
who survived starvation
in the Great Depression
the last clandestine Japanese
in the Philippines
the Korean Iron Triangle
and a terminal disease
from a liver once high on alcohol,
who now garrulous and witty
will tell you that he jogs and swims
and fucks and lives that charmed life
to which any poor boy can aspire,
is a paragon? The world conspires
to bury his secret: that old man
is scared of death.

SPECTATOR SPORT

Spindrift sifted by sails
whets salubrious gentility
and salts a troubled shore

where green eyes watch
yachtsmen without Yorick
who neither laugh nor die.

BUOYANCY

Elysium is as far as to
The very nearest Room

—Emily Dickinson

LATITUDINARIAN

My eight-year-old granddaughter
cut a Granny Smith at its equator:
"Look, Grandpa, stars live in the apple."

And there the ripening universe
set evolution's seeds from Eden on
unshrouded in this autumn twilight.

In all of sixty fact-filled years
my fancy never left the earth
to cut an apple any way but north

                            to south—

now her hemispheric eye
converts my doubts to galaxies
awaiting in my dark uncut interior.

POEM WITHOUT ENDING

No single seagull
falling against glint
of winter solstice

but rises beyond
light-years spent
in fallow hourglass

flint

for druid dreams
while ocean echoes
grace every cell

SUNDAY MATINS
(County Sligo, 1987)

Lambent sunlight echoes
seagulls from the bay uphill
to stoic passage graves

gaunt megaliths surviving
four thousand feathery years
leaving no shards or ashes

each stone an unmarked rune
for shadows sacring earth
translated by exploring seagulls

    who still refuse to die.

CODA

Autumn puffs kiss death to prisms of leaves
basking in second childhoods. Old beards
pause on grass of an Indian summer, the air
scented like spring and the maiden.

A jogger rustles illusions of air, gasping
immortality, as if delaying his translation
gives him a better chance to spawn stories
with lovers untutored in archaic tongues.

Now few chant but microchips—old joggers
keep alive their libraries, seeding for spring
against the tyranny of terminals.

IN DEFENSE OF ADAM

They scorn, "He died Jogging"
as if there were a better jaunt
to heaven—unless it's joking
or swimming or coupling flesh
of God-created quintessence.

Maybe with the risen Jesus
I'll jog from the dead, again
to join this pearl welkin
the soft surf at twilight
God's grass palming my feet—

but if I don't run hereafter
or butterfly or jest, I'll still
love, not with sport or script
but the irony of holy writ.

SUNDIAL

Air after rain limns crystal in the garden,
still and brittle, immortal for an instant,
tiny clouds pause, the sun is mirrored

in the lake where shadows rest deep
and even the lapping waters are silent
for this moment earth itself believes,

waits, while the fir seed hidden and unheard
is cuddled by rich loam or poor loam, warmed
without foreboding, beyond success or harm.

One such a morning in lush grass, a rainbow
swaddling all movement, I saw the seedling
had reached beyond my little science.

METEORA, GREECE

Twenty million years ago these sudden rocks erupted
out of the bubbling ocean—earth's barbaric yawp—
nature's skyscrapers stunning the world traveller.
Limned on the scarps are clowns, stories, hidden hells and heavens
shaped by the rising and setting sun as if no earth existed.

On these apocalyptic heights monasteries stretch
to pearl—one with sky and pinnacle.
The eye cannot clutch the vista, and even the mind
falters as it contemplates the drop to nothingness
and then aches for meaning.

Why do no Greek myths tell us of this geologic grant?
Are not the Meteora rocks useful?
For do not all myths have an economic base?
Does not myth follow politics? Were not the Greek gods
on the side with the heaviest boulders?

These rocks are too sheer to breed deer,
raise children, defend towns, or grow crops.
No land, clan, or victory is debtor to these sleeping stones—
no Artemis, Athena, Ares, or Demeter
glorifies this dormant warp of nature.

And thus it remained for centuries
unloved, unwanted, unpraised, unfeared—
till a faith found in these quickening stones
a ground between serenity and abyss.
Only God and tourists make a Meteora useful.

A GLOSS ON THE GLOAMING

That southern twilight is so spare
I only paused for fireflies
that hinted evensong's mirage

for young I fancied scribbling flints
fey novas of the solstice night
irradiant with mortality

but now prefer the seemingly eternal
with quiet purple scrawling up the hills
God's warm-up for the dark's auroral dreams.

HERITAGE

In the pitch of the Great Depression
I repressed my childhood
rebelled against my idled father

and opted for a chauvinist career
of big sticks and bottom lines
with a BB gun for shooting sparrows.

Years later dozing with crosswords,
a costless exercise for idled minds,
I sit puzzled on my father's lap

he reckons lofty haunt is aerie
spring's harbinger a swallow
and the bard of peace a dove—

his Spectre still is punning tropes—
things that go spook in the night
                      are not ghosts but owls.

DAUGHTERS OF ELYSIUM

Lambent twilight weaves

tendril into memory

hushed scent of seaweed.

THE END OF THE ICE AGE

Still air Easter moon

lithic chrysalis christens

white-fired dogwood.

LAUDS IN THE ALGARVE

Moonlit dreams echo and fade
aubades awaken the quiet
church tiles phosphoresce to blue nimbus.

At equinox in pure air
the sun breaks from Andalusia brilliant
burning the Atlantic back.

Whitewashed villas mirror light
naked from the tip of flame—
comets numinous and sudden.

Every moment of history lives
as this precious second
flashing westward to Sagres

navigated fifteen billion years
and I am caught up like Prince Henry
discovering the edge of a fresh world

as if a flint had been crossing
the abyss from nothingness
like that first incandescence.

"YOU MUST CHANGE YOUR LIFE."
—Rilke

Because detente avoids my gut
while Eden licks an ice cream cone
I throw the holy book at God

who needn't duck or throw it back
just grins and says *Did you hear the one
about Saint Anonymous*

*who threw an electric typewriter at Satan
in exchange for bytes of a computer
but still carries a macrochip on his shoulder?*

OREGON AGATE

Ten thousand years ago
with cooling basalt
a demi-god dreamily
framed this icon
as steeping colors
meandered centuries.

I cut through crust
polish the hidden core—
slant rivers blue and rust
translucent even on
an obscure light—
and plagiarize its prayer.

ASPERGES NIGHT
(for Jean Dillon)

If I christen a mizzling love
why do my erotic verses
still kindle your fancy?

If romance only lasts
seven months or so
as some psychologist said

why have I lied
declaring it eternal—
coupling, a lotus lust?

Because you and I have slept
yes, slept, together forty years
lakes of dreams interlapping

when we could spare little else,
not pastime companions
but lovers who wash each other.

BUOYANCY

I swam faster than the earth spins
cresting blue water beyond breakers
till daughter said I was half way to China

though it was only the Atlantic
and my destiny Greece and Rome.
Now I swim beyond philosophy

and the world and all the stars
spin away from my crawl
taking my shores with them

leaving me with only the self
in the dark pacific of the night,
faint, but still swimming.